WEDDING MUSIC

I. ARIA

G.F. HANDEL

2nd Violin
B-458

2nd Violin
II. BRIDAL CHORUS
(from "Lohengrin")

R. WAGNER

III. WEDDING MARCH
(from "A Midsummer Night's Dream")

F. MENDELSSOHN

IV. TRUMPET VOLUNTARY

J. CLARK

V. WINTER

(slow movement)

A. VIVALDI

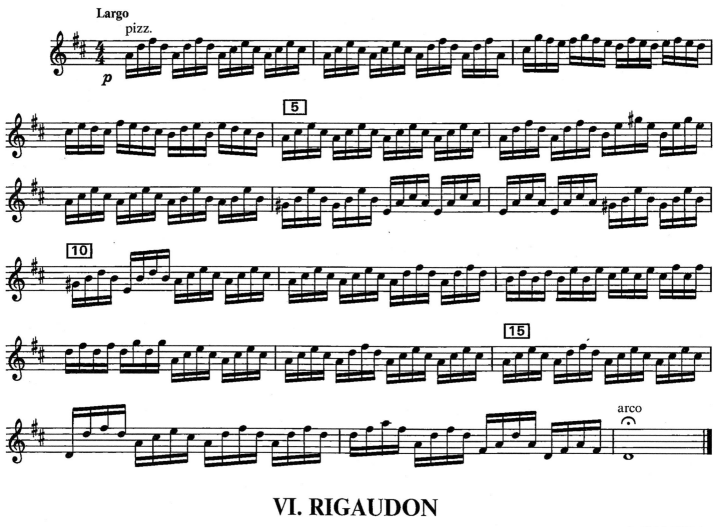

VI. RIGAUDON

A. CAMPRA

B-458

D.C. al Fine

VII. THEME FROM 1ST SYMPHONY

J. BRAHMS

Allegro non troppo

rit.

VIII. MARCH
(from "Marriage of Figaro")

W.A. MOZART

IX. TRUMPET TUNE

H. PURCELL

X. CANON

J. PACHELBEL

XI. JESU, JOY OF MAN'S DESIRING

J. S. BACH

2nd Violin

XII. WINTER
(From 1st movement)

A. VIVALDI